THREAT TO THE MONARCH BUTTERFLY

Rebecca Thatcher Murcia

Mitchell Lane
PUBLISHERS

P.O. Box 196
Hockessin, Delaware 19707
Visit us on the web: www.mitchelllane.com
Comments? email us: mitchelllane@mitchelllane.com

Printing   1   2   3   4   5   6   7   8   9

A Robbie Reader/On the Verge of Extinction: Crisis in the Environment

Frogs in Danger
Polar Bears on the Hudson Bay
The Snows of Kilimanjaro
Threat to Ancient Egyptian Treasures
Threat to the Monarch Butterfly

Library of Congress Cataloging-in-Publication Data
Murcia, Rebecca Thatcher, 1962-
  Threat to the monarch butterfly / by Rebecca Thatcher Murcia.
    p. cm. — (A Robbie reader)
  Includes bibliographical references and index.
  ISBN-13: 978-1-58415-587-4 (library bound)
  1. Monarch butterfly—Juvenile literature. I. Title.
  QL561.D3M865 2007
  595.78'9—dc22
                                                                              2007000819

ABOUT THE AUTHOR: Rebecca Thatcher Murcia graduated from the University of Massachusetts at Amherst and worked as a newspaper reporter for fifteen years. She lives with her two sons in Akron, Pennsylvania. Among her other books for Mitchell Lane Publishers are *The Civil Rights Movement, E.B. White,* and *Carl Sandburg.*

PHOTO CREDITS: Cover, pp. 4, 10, 18—Jupiterimages Corporation; p. 6—Jonathan Scott; p. 15—Barbara Page; pp. 8, 12, 13—Armon; p. 7—Sweet Briar College; pp. 9, 16,—Dr. Lincoln Brower; pp. 20, 22—Adrian Shelley; p. 24—The Project Pro Cosara

PLB

TABLE OF CONTENTS

Words in **bold** type can be found in the glossary.

EXTINCTION

Monarch butterflies fly from Canada and the United States to the mountains of Central Mexico every year. They can fly as far as 100 miles in a day.

Chapter One

THE INCREDIBLE INSECT

Go outside on a fall day almost anywhere in the eastern United States or Canada, and you might see an orange, yellow, and black butterfly go by. The graceful little insect is probably on an incredible journey. Monarch butterflies from eastern Canada and the United States usually live only about six weeks. But every fall a kind of super group of millions and millions of monarch butterflies lives for about eight months. They fly all the way to the mountains of Central Mexico, **hibernate** there over the winter, then fly back north to lay eggs. West coast monarchs also **migrate** from the mountains to the coast of central California, but that journey

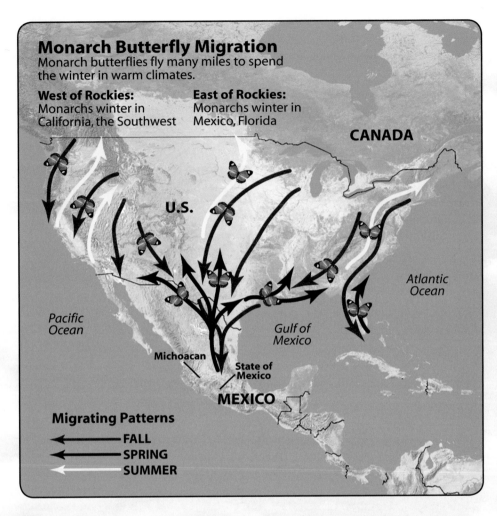

Monarch Butterfly Migration
Monarch butterflies fly many miles to spend the winter in warm climates.

West of Rockies:
Monarchs winter in California, the Southwest

East of Rockies:
Monarchs winter in Mexico, Florida

CANADA

U.S.

Atlantic Ocean

Pacific Ocean

Gulf of Mexico

Michoacan

State of Mexico

MEXICO

Migrating Patterns
← —— FALL
← —— SPRING
← —— SUMMER

The main monarch butterfly migration extends for more than a thousand miles across North America to Mexico. Smaller populations also migrate to Florida and to the coast of California.

is not as long as the journey of eastern monarchs.

The monarch's amazing system for surviving cold North American winters makes its life cycle unlike that of any other insect.

People find it hard to believe that these tiny animals find their way to the same remote mountains of Central Mexico, even though, unlike birds, they did not go the previous year with their parents. When they arrive in Mexico, they cluster together on tall **oyamel** pine trees in remote forests and wait for spring. Sometimes so many butterflies huddle together on a particular branch that it bends under the combined weight of the butterflies. Whole trees are often covered with the colorful insects.

The oyamel trees of the high mountains of Central Mexico provide a place where monarch butterflies can stay warm and dry as they cling together through the winter. When spring comes, and the butterflies will begin their journey north.

The amazing monarch butterfly begins life as a tiny egg laid on a milkweed plant. A butterfly larva, or caterpillar, will hatch from each egg.

The orange coloring on the trees at the center of this picture shows the presence of thousands of monarch butterflies. They huddle together for warmth during the cold—but not usually freezing—winters of the Central Mexican high mountains.

In the spring, when it's warm enough to go north again, they take off in spectacular orange, black, and yellow clouds. The sound of so many butterfly wings beating makes a noise like a strong gust of wind. They fly north in search of flowers with **nectar** they can eat. They look for milkweed plants on which to lay their eggs. The way these insects travel and survive has made them popular among people, but their traveling patterns put them at risk.

The monarch caterpillars eat and grow and shed their skin at a surprising speed. After they have eaten enough leaves, they will attach themselves to the underside of the plant and begin to change into butterflies.

THE MONARCH LIFE CYCLE

Like most butterflies, monarchs start their lives as tiny caterpillars, or **larvae** (LAR-vee). The larvae hatch from eggs their mothers have laid on milkweed plants. From almost the moment they are born, the caterpillars become little eating machines. First they eat the shell of the egg they were in. Then they eat the leaves on which they were laid. They eat and grow, and eat and grow. Then they eat and grow some more. When they grow too big for their skin, they shed it. An under layer of skin will then harden. This process is known as molting. They molt five times during the larval stage, which can take from nine to fourteen days.

In the next stage, a larva will fasten itself to a plant. It will spin a pad of silk onto the plant, then it will change into a sac known as a **pupa** (PYOO-puh). The pupa grabs onto the silk pad with dozens of tiny hooks. The pupa forms a hard shell known as a **chrysalis** (KRIH-sah-lis). Inside the chrysalis, the larva gradually changes into a butterfly.

This process of changing is called **metamorphosis** (meh-tuh-MOR-fuh-sis). It can take as long as two weeks. When the butterfly first emerges, it will stand still and stretch out its wings to let them dry.

To change into a butterfly, the caterpillar will attach itself to the bottom of a leaf. Then it will grow a sac and become a pupa.

The hardened pupa is called the chrysalis (left). After about two weeks inside the chrysalis, the fully developed butterfly slowly emerges (right).

Usually, the butterflies are ready to mate soon after emerging from the chrysalis. The males and females mate, and each female grows hundreds of tiny eggs. For about three out of four generations, the butterflies die about six weeks after mating. But every fourth generation, known as the **Methuselah** (meh-THOOZ-uh-leh) generation, lives for about eight months. The Methuselah generation is usually born in late August or September. Unlike their parents, grandparents, and great-grandparents, they cannot mate right away.

Instead, they begin the long journey south to Mexico.

They fly during the day, and at night they stop to eat nectar from flowers and rest. After about three weeks of travel, they arrive in the high mountains of Central Mexico, mostly in the state of Michoacan (mee-choh-ah-KAHN). They hibernate amid the oyamel fir trees there. The winters are cold, but the thick clumps of trees keep them from freezing.

In the spring, the butterflies are able to mate. The female butterflies fly north, looking for milkweed plants on which they can lay their eggs. The butterflies, their children, and their grandchildren will continue the journey north. For example, the butterflies that hibernated in Mexico may get as far as Texas. Their children might fly to North Carolina, and their children may go all the way to New England or Canada. When September rolls around again, it is time to fly back to Mexico.

Scientists have studied the monarch migration for years and years, but they still do

The milkweed that monarch caterpillars eat contains a poison called **cardiac glycoside**. It makes the butterflies taste terrible, so birds do not eat them.

not understand exactly how butterflies find the same forests in Central Mexico that their great-grandparents used for the winter. They think the butterflies might use the sun or the earth's **magnetism** to navigate.

EXTINCTION

Migrating monarch butterflies—just like long travelers everywhere—get thirsty and need to drink. They fly down to streams to quench their thirst.

A LIFE CYCLE UNDER THREAT

Unlike other species that are **endangered**, there are still millions and millions of monarch butterflies flying to Mexico every year. Usually, before scientists declare an animal to be endangered, there has to be proof that the animal's population is declining. The Florida panther, for example, is endangered because there are only between 30 and 50 still alive in the wild. While the monarch butterflies probably number in the billions, scientists consider the monarch to be in danger.

The Mexican government has made it illegal to cut down trees in a large area where the monarch butterflies spend the winter.

During their migration, monarch butterflies stop to eat and rest. The butterflies need lots of nectar to get enough strength for their long flight.

In 1986 it created a butterfly preserve that covers more than 56,000 **hectares** (216 square miles) in the states of Michoacan and Mexico. (Mexico is the name of a state within Mexico. It is to the east of Michoacan). However, illegal loggers continue to cut down and sell the wood to woodworking companies. Peasants, or the local people who have few opportunities for work, also cut down the trees for fuel for their homes.

Some local people support the preserve. They earn money from the tourists who come to see the butterflies. But others are angry. One illegal logger, who had covered his face with mud to hide his identity, told a newspaper reporter: "Everyone worries about the butterflies. What about us?"

The monarch butterflies' life cycle is also threatened in the United States and Canada. Milkweed, which used to be plentiful along the edges of fields and roads throughout North America, is becoming less common. Farmland is used to create into housing developments, highways, and other projects at a rate of almost 3,000 acres a day in the United States. Farmers, who need to get as much crops as possible from their land, use **herbicides** (ER-beh-syds) to kill milkweed in their fields. Highway departments also spray roadsides with weed killer.

The monarch butterfly migration is at risk, but people in at least three countries are trying to help.

EXTINCTION

At Highland Elementary School in Ephrata, Pennsylvania, students have created a monarch waystation where they can observe the monarch butterfly.

HELPING THE MONARCH

Students at Highland Elementary School in Ephrata (EH-frah-tuh), Pennsylvania, are among the thousands of people who are trying to save the monarch butterfly. They have set up a **waystation**, or a place where the butterflies can stop to lay their eggs, and where the larvae can eat. Adrian Shelley, a fifth-grade teacher at the school, said the students were thrilled to see how quickly the monarch butterflies arrived on the milkweed the students had planted. The students searched for larvae and brought some of them into their classroom to raise. It was surprising to see how much milkweed each larva could eat every day—usually one

Tiny tags attached to the monarch butterfly's wings help scientists keep track of the monarch migration.

large leaf or a few smaller leaves. Once the butterflies emerged, the students tagged them and released them back into the wild.

All across the United States and Canada, schools, home gardeners, and other organizations are planting gardens specially designed to give monarch butterflies a place to eat and reproduce. "We are trying to find out as much as we can, but we are also trying to protect them," Mr. Shelley said.

Monarch Watch, the organization at the University of Kansas that sponsors the monarch waystation program, also wants people who care about butterflies to push their governments for change. According to Monarch Watch, monarch supporters need to get city and state governments to stop spraying herbicides on milkweed plants growing along roadsides.

In Mexico, the government has made the monarch preserve bigger in order to provide more natural areas for the butterflies to roost during the winter. **Environmentalists** (en-veye-run-MEN-tuh-lists) from the United States and Mexico are trying to help local people find ways to survive in the forest without cutting down the trees needed by the butterflies. It is not enough to simply pass laws saying that people cannot cut down the trees, said Eduardo Rendon, a scientist with the World Wildlife Fund in Mexico. Local people and environmentalists must work

The Mexican government has banned logging in the forests that the monarch butterflies use the most, but there is a lot of demand for wood, and the government cannot enforce its own rules.

together to help people find other ways of surviving. "We cannot have conservation at all costs," Rendon said.

Many of the local people are trying to protect the trees from illegal logging. In El Paso, Armando Sanchez Martinez passed out weapons to residents who were willing to go on armed patrols to protect the trees. "The illegal loggers wanted to shoot one of us to frighten us and take our forest," Sanchez told a newspaper reporter. "Now they are going to have to shoot us all."

Fighting back with weapons is not really the best way to solve the conflict. Enforcing the law and finding ways that people can live near the forest without damaging it are better solutions. There are many organizations trying to do that. One example is Eco-life, an organization from California. It has given 400 new ovens to people who live near the monarch preserve. The ovens reduce the amount of wood need for heating and cooking. They will make it easier for the locals to live without taking wood illegally.

Even with so many people trying to help the monarch butterfly, more needs to be done to help save its migration route. Only then will the monarch butterfly survive.

Life Cycle of the Monarch Butterfly

1. Eggs are laid
2. Larvae feed on leaves
3. Beginning of pupa stage
4. Chrysalis
5. Butterfly emerging
6. Butterfly ready for first flight
7. Adult monarch butterfly

Create Your Own Butterfly Waystation

A monarch butterfly waystation at your home or school will not only help the monarch butterflies, it will also be fun and educational. Get an adult to help you. You can order a Monarch Waystation kit by calling (800) 780-9986 or by going on line at Shop.MonarchWatch.org. Read the instructions in the kit and plant your monarch garden. If you want your waystation to be counted, you can fill out a form, pay a small fee, and get a certification from Monarch Watch.

Get Involved in the Political Process

Politicians can pass laws that will help save the monarch butterfly, but they need to know how important it is. You can call, visit, or write to your representative. The letter can read:

> Dear Member of Congress,
> I think the government needs to do more to protect the monarch butterfly migration. Please work to stop the use of herbicides that kill milkweed and other plants the butterflies need. Our government should also do what it can to stop logging in the Monarch Butterfly Preserve in Mexico.
> (Then include some detail about yourself)
>
> Sincerely,
> (your name here)

The names and addresses of your lawmakers are available at www.house.gov or www.senate.gov. From the home page, click on "Representatives" or "Senators."

Organize a Fundraiser

The organizations working to save the monarch butterfly can always use money. Pick one of the organizations working on monarch preservation and raise money for it. You can hold a bake sale, a trash drive, or a walk-a-thon. Log on to www.ecolifefoundation.org or www.worldwildlife.org to find out how to donate the money to help the monarchs.

Books

Bredeson, Carmen. *Monarch Butterflies Up Close*. Berkeley Heights, New Jersey: Enslow Publishers, Inc., 2006.

Gibbons, Gail. *The Monarch Butterfly*. New York: Holiday House, 1989.

Himmelman, John. *A Monarch Butterfly's Life*. New York: Children's Press, 1999.

Mikula, Rick. *The Family Butterfly Book: Discover the Joy of Attracting, Raising & Nurturing Butterflies*. Vermont: Storey Books, 2000.

Murray, Julia. *Monarch Butterflies (Life Cycles)*. Edina, Minnesota: Buddy Books, 2007.

Works Consulted

Durkin, Pat. "Migrating Monarch Butterfly." *National Geographic News*, November 22, 2000. http://news.nationalgeographic.com/news/2000/11/1122_monarchs.html

Halpern, Sue. *Four Wings and a Prayer: Caught in the Mystery of the Monarch Butterfly*. New York: Random House, 2002.

The Journey North: Monarch Butterfly http://www.learner.org/jnorth/monarch/

McKinley, James C., Jr. "Chain Saw Thins Flocks of Migrants on Gold Wings." *The New York Times*, March 12, 2005, p. A4.

Oberhauser, Karen S. *The Monarch Butterfly: Biology and Conservation*. New York: Cornell University, 2004.

Roos, Daniel. "Battle Royal Over Monarch Habitat; Illegal Logging by Armed Gangs a Big Threat to Villages, Butterfly Reserve in Mexico." *San Francisco Chronicle*, August 23, 2004, p. A4. http://www.sfgate.com/cgi-bin/article.cgi?file=/c/a/2004/08/23/MNGLC8CNVHI.DTL

Sherwood, Dave. "Amazing Monarch Butterflies in Full Force in Maine This Summer." *Kennebec Journal*, August 26, 2006, p. D1.

Thompson, Ginger. "Where Butterflies Rest, Damage Runs Rampant." *The New York Times*, June 2, 2004, p. A11.

FIND OUT MORE

Wiley, Judy. "Monarch Butterflies Descend Like Clouds on Mexico Sanctuaries." *Pittsburgh Post-Gazette*, August 20, 2006, p. E4.

On the Internet

The Eco-Life Foundation; Monarch Butterflies
http://www.ecolifefoundation.org/ECOmonarchsl.html

The Monarch Butterfly Journey North for Kids http://www.learner.org/jnorth/tm/monarch/jr/KidsJourneyNorth.html

Monarch Watch www.monarchwatch.org

The North American Butterfly Association http://www.naba.org/

Rick Mikula, the Butterfly Guy www.butterflyrick.com

World Wildlife Fund: Monarchs http://worldwildlife.org/monarchs/

GLOSSARY

cardiac glycoside (KAR-dee-ak GLEYE-koh-syd)—a substance found in milkweed that poisons the heart of birds, fish, and mammals.

chrysalis (KRIH-sah-lis)—the firm case that encloses the pupa.

endangered (in-DAYN-jerd)—in a dangerous situation; at risk of dying out.

environmentalist (en-veye-run-MEN-tuh-list)—a person who is concerned about protecting things in the natural world, such as plants, animals, and rivers and streams.

GLOSSARY

hectare (HEK-tayr)—a unit of measurement for land equal to 10,000 square meters, or about 2.47 acres.

herbicide (ER-beh-syd)—a poison used to kill plants.

hibernate (HEYE-ber-nayt)—to pass the winter in a resting state, with body functions slowed.

larva (LAR-vuh)—The caterpillar-like second stage of a butterfly's life. Plural form is **larvae** (LAR-vee).

magnetism (MAG-nuh-tism)—the ability to attract certain substances, especially metals.

metamorphosis (meh-tuh-MOR-fuh-sis)—a complete change of an animal.

Methuselah (meh-THOOZ-uh-leh)—a character in the Bible who lived to be 969 years old.

migrate (MEYE-grayt)—to move from one area to another in search of food or better climate.

nectar—a sweet liquid produced by flowers.

oyamel (OY-ah-mel)—the type of fir tree that grows in the high mountains of Central Mexico and are the preferred winter roosting trees of the monarch butterfly.

pupa (PYOO-puh)—the third stage of a butterfly's life, during which the insect changes from a larva to a butterfly. Plural form is **pupae** (PYOO-pee).

waystation (WAY-stay-shun)—a place where butterflies can stop along their migration route to eat or lay their eggs.